This book was compiled by Daniel Melehi with the A.I assistance of Inventabot

Dedication

I hope this helps all of my wonderful readers achieve all their goals in their business. And I would like to thank my wonderful wife for all of her continued support in all my ventures.

©Daniel Melehi

May 7 2023

Contents

Chapter 1: Introduction to Java..........................7

Subchapter 1.1: Java History and Development.............7

Subchapter 1.2: Java Installation and Setup 8

Subchapter 1.3: Java Syntax and Structure 9

Subchapter 1.4: The Java Standard Library 9

Java History and Development..................................10

Java Installation and Setup..12

Java Syntax and Structure 13

    Java Syntax 14

    Java Structure 14

    Conclusion 15

The Java Standard Library 16

Object-Oriented Programming Basics 17

Classes and Objects...18

Inheritance and Polymorphism 19

Abstraction and Encapsulation 20

Interfaces and Abstract Classes 22

Classes and Objects...24

Inheritance and Polymorphism 26

Abstraction and Encapsulation 27

Subchapter 2.4: Interfaces and Abstract Classes............28

Chapter 3: Exception Handling and Debugging 30

Subchapter 3.1: Handling Exceptions in Java 30

Subchapter 3.2: Debugging Techniques and Tools 31

Subchapter 3.3: Best Practices for Exception Handling and Debugging 32

Handling Exceptions in Java.. 33

Subchapter 3.2: Debugging Techniques and Tools 34

Best Practices for Exception Handling and Debugging..... 36

Chapter 4: Java Collections Framework 38

Subchapter 4.1: Lists, Sets, and Maps 39

Subchapter 4.2: Iterators and Generics 39

Subchapter 4.3: Sorting and Searching Techniques.......... 40

Lists, Sets, and Maps 41

Iterators and Generics.. 43

Subchapter 4.3: Sorting and Searching Techniques.......... 45
Sorting Techniques 45
Searching Techniques 46

Chapter 5: Multithreading and Concurrency 47

Subchapter 5.1: Threads and Processes in Java............... 48

Subchapter 5.2: Thread Synchronization Mechanisms 49

Subchapter 5.3: Concurrent Programming Best Practices 50

Threads and Processes in Java.. 51

Thread Synchronization Mechanisms 52

Concurrent Programming Best Practices 54
    1. Avoid Shared Mutable State 55
    2. Keep Critical Sections Small 55
    3. Use Thread Pools 56
    4. Use Atomic Variables and Synchronization Primitives 57
    5. Test Your Code Thoroughly 57

Subchapter 6.1: File Input-Output Operations in Java 60

Subchapter 6.2: JDBC Programming and Database Integration 63
    Connecting to a Database 63
    Executing SQL Statements 65
    Using Prepared Statements 66
    Conclusion 68

Object-Relational Mapping with Hibernate 68

Chapter 7: Java Networking and Security 70

Subchapter 7.1: Socket Programming in Java 71
    Handling Exceptions in Networking 71
    Multi-threading in Networking 72
    Encoding/Decoding Data in Networking 72

Subchapter 7.2: Securing Java Applications with Cryptography 73
    Best Practices for Java Security 74

Socket Programming in Java 74

Securing Java Applications with Cryptography 76

Best Practices for Java Security 78
    1. Keep Java Updated 78
    2. Use Secure Coding Practices 79

  3. Use Encryption for Sensitive Data 79
  4. Limit Access to Sensitive Resources 79
  5. Implement Access Controls 80
  6. Use SSL/TLS for Network Communications 80
  7. Regularly Conduct Security Audits 81

Chapter 8: Java Web Development *81*

Introduction to Web Technologies 82
  HTML and CSS: 82
  JavaScript: 82
  Servlets and JSP Programming: 83
  Web Services: 83

Servlets and JSP Programming 83

Web Services with RESTful APIs 84

Introduction to Web Technologies 85

Servlets and JSP Programming 87

Subchapter 8.3: Web Services with RESTful APIs 88

Chapter 9: Design Patterns and Best Practices *90*

Subchapter 9.1: Gang of Four Design Patterns 90
  The Singleton Pattern 91
  The Factory Method Pattern 92
  The Observer Pattern 92

Subchapter 9.2: Architectural Patterns and Best Practices
.... 93
  The Model-View-Controller Pattern 94
  Layered Architecture 94
  Microservices 95

Subchapter 9.3: Java Code Refactoring Techniques 95

    Extract Method 96

    Extract Class 96

    Replace Conditional with Polymorphism 97

Architectural Patterns and Best Practices 101

Java Code Refactoring Techniques 103

    Why Refactor Java Code? 104

    When Should You Refactor Your Java Code? 104

    Types of Refactoring Techniques 105

    Best Practices for Refactoring Java Code 106

Chapter 10: Java Performance Optimization *108*

Subchapter 10.1: Java Memory Management and Performance 108

Subchapter 10.2: Profiling and Tuning Java Applications 109

Subchapter 10.3: Best Practices for Java Performance Optimization 110

Java Memory Management and Performance 111

Profiling and Tuning Java Applications 113

Chapter 1: Introduction to Java

Java is an extremely popular and versatile programming language used for developing a wide range of applications. In this chapter, we will cover everything you need to know to get started with Java, from its history and development to installation and setup.

SUBCHAPTER 1.1: JAVA HISTORY AND DEVELOPMENT

Java was created in the mid-1990s by James Gosling, Patrick Naughton, and others at Sun Microsystems. Originally developed as a language for interactive television, Java quickly became popular for internet applications due to its ability to run on any platform with a Java Virtual Machine

(JVM). Over the years, Java has evolved to become a robust and versatile programming language, used in everything from mobile applications to large-scale enterprise systems. Its popularity and ubiquity continue to grow, making it an important language to learn for aspiring developers.

SUBCHAPTER 1.2: JAVA INSTALLATION AND SETUP

To get started with Java development, you'll need to install the appropriate software and tools on your computer. This typically involves downloading and installing the Java Development Kit (JDK) and an Integrated Development Environment (IDE) such as Eclipse or IntelliJ. Once you have the necessary software installed, you can create a new Java project and start writing code. Java syntax and structure can be somewhat different from other languages, so it's important to take the time to learn the basics.

SUBCHAPTER 1.3: JAVA SYNTAX AND STRUCTURE

Java is known for its strict syntax and structure, which can initially be challenging for new developers to learn. However, the payoff is a language that is powerful, flexible, and reliable. Java code is organized into classes, which contain methods and other code blocks. Variables must be explicitly declared and initialized, and strict data typing is enforced. Understanding these basic concepts is crucial to becoming a proficient Java developer.

SUBCHAPTER 1.4: THE JAVA STANDARD LIBRARY

One of the great strengths of Java is its extensive standard library, which provides a wide variety of pre-written code and functionality. Examples include the Collections Framework, which provides data structures like lists and maps, and the

Java Networking API, which supports complex networking protocols. As a Java developer, understanding and utilizing these standard libraries is essential for efficient and effective programming. Once you have a solid understanding of the basics, you'll be ready to dive deeper into the world of Java development.

JAVA HISTORY AND DEVELOPMENT

Java is a popular programming language that has been around for over two decades. It was developed by James Gosling and his team at Sun Microsystems in the early 1990s. The language was first released to the public in 1995, under the name "Oak." It was later renamed to "Java" due to trademark issues. The original goal of Java was to create a language that could run on multiple platforms. This was accomplished by using a "write once, run anywhere" approach. This meant that code written in Java could be compiled and run on any machine that had a Java Virtual Machine (JVM) installed. Over the years, Java has evolved significantly. New features have been added, and older features have been improved. Today, Java is used for a wide variety of applications, ranging from mobile apps to enterprise-level software systems. One of the major strengths of Java is its robustness. The language includes built-in error handling mechanisms that help to prevent crashes and other unexpected behavior. Additionally, Java's object-oriented design makes it easy to write and maintain large, complex programs. Overall, Java has had a significant impact on the world of programming. Its "write once, run anywhere" approach has made it a popular choice for developers who need to create cross-platform applications. As the language continues to evolve, it will likely remain an important tool for developers for years to come.

JAVA INSTALLATION AND SETUP

Before beginning your journey with Java, it is necessary to install Java Development Kit (JDK) onto your computer. To get started, visit the official Oracle website and download the latest version of JDK for your operating system. Once the download is completed, follow the installation instructions to install it on your machine. After installing JDK, you need to set the JAVA_HOME environment variable on your computer. This variable tells your computer where Java is installed and allows your machine to recognize Java commands. To set the JAVA_HOME environment variable, follow these steps: 1. Open the system properties window on your computer. 2. Click on the Advanced tab. 3. Click on the Environment Variables button. 4. Under System Variables, click the New button. 5. Set the Variable name to JAVA_HOME. 6. Set the Variable value to the path where JDK is installed on your computer. You also need to add the JDK bin directory to your system's Path variable to be able to execute Java commands from anywhere on your computer. To add the JDK bin directory to your system's Path variable, follow these steps: 1. Open the System Properties window on your computer. 2. Click on the Advanced tab. 3. Click on the Environment Variables button. 4. Scroll down to the System Variables section and select the Path variable. 5. Click on Edit. 6. Click on New and add the path to your JDK bin directory. By following these steps, you should now have Java installed and setup on your computer. You are now ready to start coding with Java!

JAVA SYNTAX AND STRUCTURE

Java is a programming language that is known for its simplicity and ease of use. In this subchapter, we will discuss the syntax and structure of Java to help you get started with the language.

Java Syntax

Java code is written in plain text and is saved with a .java file extension. The basic syntax of Java includes keywords, identifiers, operators, and statements. Keywords are reserved words that have a specific meaning and cannot be used as identifiers. Examples of keywords in Java include "public," "static," and "void." Identifiers are names given to variables, methods, classes, and other entities in Java. Identifiers cannot begin with a number and cannot be a keyword. Operators are symbols that perform actions on operands. Examples of operators in Java include the plus sign (+) for addition and the equal sign (=) for assignment. Statements are lines of code that perform actions or make decisions. Examples of statements in Java include "if" and "for" statements.

Java Structure

Java programs are structured in classes, which contain methods and variables. A class is defined using the "class" keyword, followed by the class name. Methods are blocks of code that perform a specific task. They are defined within a class and can be accessed by objects of that class. Methods can be either static or non-static. Variables are used to store data within a program. They are declared using a data type and a name, and can be given a value using the equals sign (=). Java programs are executed from a main method, which must be declared within a class. The main method is the entry point for the program, and is where the program begins executing.

Conclusion

Understanding the syntax and structure of Java is fundamental to writing effective and efficient code. In the next subchapter, we will discuss the Java Standard Library and its many built-in classes and methods that make programming in Java even easier.

THE JAVA STANDARD LIBRARY

The Java Standard Library is a comprehensive collection of pre-written Java code that provides developers with a foundation for building Java applications. It contains a vast array of classes and interfaces for everything from basic input/output operations to complex data structures. One of the primary benefits of using the Java Standard Library is that it saves developers a significant amount of time. Instead of writing classes from scratch to handle common operations, they can use code that's already been written and tested. Additionally, the Java Standard Library promotes consistency across different Java applications, which makes it easier for developers to read and understand code written by others. Some of the most commonly used classes in the Java Standard Library include: - java.lang: This package contains fundamental classes that are necessary for the Java programming language to function, such as Object and String. - java.util: This package contains classes for handling collections, dates, times, and other utility classes. - java.io: This package contains classes for performing input/output operations, such as reading from and writing to files. - java.net: This package contains classes for working with network connections. The Java Standard Library is constantly evolving, with new classes and interfaces added with every new version of Java. As a Java developer, it's essential to stay up-to-date with these changes to take full advantage of the library's capabilities.

Object-Oriented Programming Basics

Object-oriented programming (OOP) is a powerful programming paradigm that allows developers to create applications in a way that models real-world objects, making them easier to understand, maintain, and modify. In this chapter, we will explore the basic principles of OOP, including classes, objects, inheritance, polymorphism, and more.

CLASSES AND OBJECTS

In OOP, a class is a blueprint for creating objects. It defines the properties and behaviors that an object of that class will have. An object, on the other hand, is an instance of a class. It has specific values for its properties and can perform actions as defined by the class. To create a class in Java, we use the `class` keyword, followed by the class name, and then use curly braces to define its properties and methods. Here's an example: ```java public class Person { // properties String name; int age; // constructor public Person(String name, int age) { this.name = name; this.age = age; } // method public void sayHello() { System.out.println("Hello, my name is " + name); } } ``` In this example, we've defined a `Person` class with two properties (`name` and `age`), a constructor to set those properties when a new `Person` object is created, and a `sayHello()` method to print a greeting to the console. To create a new `Person` object, we can use the `new` keyword and pass in values for the constructor: ```java Person john = new Person("John", 30); john.sayHello(); // output: "Hello, my name is John" ```

INHERITANCE AND POLYMORPHISM

Inheritance allows classes to inherit properties and methods from other classes. This can help reduce code duplication and make it easier to organize related classes. To define a class that inherits from another class in Java, we use the `extends` keyword, followed by the name of the class we want to inherit from. ```java public class Student extends Person { int gradeLevel; public Student(String name, int age, int gradeLevel) { super(name, age); // call the constructor of the parent class this.gradeLevel = gradeLevel; } } ``` In this example, we've defined a `Student` class that inherits from the `Person` class we defined earlier. The `Student` class adds a new property (`gradeLevel`) and has its own constructor that calls the parent class constructor using the `super` keyword. Polymorphism allows objects to be treated as their parent class or any interface they implement. This can be useful for writing more flexible and reusable code. For example: ```java Person student = new Student("Jane", 16, 11); student.sayHello(); // output: "Hello, my name is Jane" ``` In this example, we've created a `Student` object but assigned it to a variable of type `Person`. This allows us to call the `sayHello()` method even though it's not defined in the `Student` class itself.

ABSTRACTION AND ENCAPSULATION

Abstraction and encapsulation are two important principles in OOP that help make code more maintainable and less error-prone. Abstraction refers to the process of hiding unnecessary details and exposing only what's necessary for other parts of the application to use. This can be achieved in Java using interfaces or abstract classes. Encapsulation refers to the process of protecting the internal state of an object and only allowing access to it through defined methods. This can help prevent unintended changes to the object's state and make it easier to change the implementation details later on. ```java public abstract class Animal { private String name; public Animal(String name) { this.name = name; } public abstract void makeSound(); public String getName() { return this.name; } } public class Dog extends Animal { public Dog(String name) { super(name); } public void makeSound() {

System.out.println("Woof!"); } } ``` In this example, we've defined an abstract `Animal` class with a private `name` property and two methods - an abstract `makeSound()` method that all `Animal` subclasses must implement, and a `getName()` method that exposes the `name` property without allowing direct access to it. The `Dog` class extends `Animal` and provides its own implementation of the `makeSound()` method.

INTERFACES AND ABSTRACT CLASSES

Interfaces and abstract classes are both used for abstraction in Java. An interface is a contract that specifies a set of methods that a class must implement. It allows for multiple inheritance and can be used to define a common behavior that multiple classes can implement. ```java public interface Drawable { void draw(); } public class Circle implements Drawable { public void draw() { // implementation details } } public class Square implements Drawable { public void draw() { // implementation details } } ``` In this example, we've defined a `Drawable` interface with a single `draw()` method. The `Circle` and `Square` classes both implement the `Drawable` interface and provide their own implementations of the `draw()` method. An abstract class is similar to an interface but can provide default implementations of methods and can also have state and constructors. ```java public abstract class Shape { private int x; private int y; public Shape(int x, int y) { this.x = x; this.y = y; } public int getX() { return this.x; } public int getY() { return this.y; } public abstract void draw(); } public class Circle extends Shape { private int radius; public Circle(int x, int y, int radius) { super(x, y); this.radius = radius; } public void draw() { // implementation details } } ``` In this example, we've defined an abstract `Shape` class with `x` and `y` properties and a constructor to set those properties. The `Shape` class also has an abstract `draw()` method that any subclass must implement. The `Circle` class extends `Shape` and adds its own `radius` property and constructor. It also provides its own implementation of the `draw()` method. In conclusion, understanding the principles of OOP is crucial for building maintainable, scalable, and extensible applications in Java. Whether you're creating new classes, inheriting from existing ones, or defining interfaces and abstract classes, keeping these concepts in mind will help you write better code.

CLASSES AND OBJECTS

Java is an object-oriented programming language, which means that every program you write in Java revolves around objects and their interactions. An object in Java is a complex data structure that combines data and behavior. We define objects in Java by creating classes. A class is a blueprint for creating objects. It describes the state of an object and the operations that can be performed on that state. A class can contain data members (class variables and instance variables) and methods (functions). To create an object in Java, we use the keyword `new`. For example, if we have a class `Person`, we can create an object of type `Person` using the following code: ``` Person myPerson = new Person(); ``` This creates a new instance of the `Person` class and assigns it to the variable `myPerson`. We can then use the methods and data members defined in the `Person` class to interact with this object. One important concept in object-oriented programming is encapsulation. Encapsulation is the practice of hiding the internal details of an object and only exposing a public interface. This allows us to change the implementation of an object without affecting the rest of the program. To achieve encapsulation in Java, we use access modifiers. Access modifiers are keywords that determine the visibility and accessibility of a class, method, or variable. There are four access modifiers in Java: - `public` - visible to all classes - `private` - visible only to the class that declares it - `protected` - visible to the class that declares it and its subclasses - default (no modifier) - visible to the class that declares it and other classes in the same package It's important to use access modifiers to control the visibility of your classes, methods, and variables, so that you can protect the internal state of your objects and prevent unintended behavior. In the next subchapter, we'll discuss inheritance and polymorphism, two important concepts in object-oriented programming.

INHERITANCE AND POLYMORPHISM

Inheritance is a powerful feature in object-oriented programming that allows one class to inherit the properties and methods of another class. The parent class is also known as the superclass, while the child class is known as the subclass. When a subclass inherits from a superclass, it can access all the non-private members of the superclass, such as attributes and methods.

In other words, the subclass inherits the behavior and capabilities of the superclass. Polymorphism, on the other hand, is a concept that refers to the ability of a variable, function, or object to take on many forms. In Java, polymorphism is implemented through inheritance and interfaces. A subclass can override or overload methods inherited from its superclass or interface, providing its own implementation. This allows for more flexibility and extensibility in code design and allows for more dynamic behavior at runtime. Understanding inheritance and polymorphism is essential for creating more modular and maintainable code. By having a solid understanding of these concepts, you can design your classes and hierarchies in a way that makes them more flexible and adaptable to changing requirements.

ABSTRACTION AND ENCAPSULATION

Abstraction and encapsulation are two important concepts in object-oriented programming that help in creating secure and maintainable code. Abstraction is the concept of hiding unnecessary details and showing only the necessary information to the outside world. In Java, abstraction is achieved using abstract classes and interfaces. Abstract classes are classes that cannot be instantiated and are used as templates for other concrete classes to inherit from. Interfaces, on the other hand, are contracts that specify a set of methods that implementing classes should provide. Encapsulation is the process of wrapping related data and behaviors together, and restricting access to the data from outside the class. In Java, encapsulation is implemented by defining the class variables as private and providing getters and setters methods to access them. The main advantage of encapsulation is that it ensures that the internal state of an object is always in a valid state when accessed through public methods. This helps in preventing unexpected behavior and improves the maintainability of the code. In summary, abstraction and encapsulation are key concepts in Java that help in creating secure and maintainable code by providing a clear separation of concerns and by hiding implementation details from the outside world.

SUBCHAPTER 2.4: INTERFACES AND ABSTRACT CLASSES

In Java, an interface is a reference type that defines a set of methods without implementation. It allows us to separate the definition of a method from its implementation. Interfaces play a vital role in achieving abstraction. Abstract classes, on the other hand, are classes that contain one or more abstract methods, which are methods without implementation. A class can inherit from an abstract class and implement its abstract methods. Abstract classes can be used to achieve both abstraction and inheritance. Using interfaces and abstract classes can make our code more modular, flexible, and easy to maintain. Interfaces are used to define a contract that a class implementing it must follow, while abstract classes are used to provide common functionality to its subclasses. One of the main differences between interfaces and abstract classes is that a class can implement multiple interfaces, but it can only inherit from a single abstract class. Another difference is that abstract classes can have constructor methods, while interfaces cannot. When designing our application, it is essential to choose the right approach, whether we need to define a set of methods or provide common functionality for our classes. Proper use of interfaces and abstract classes can lead to more readable and reusable code, which is essential for creating robust applications.

Chapter 3: Exception Handling and Debugging

When writing code in Java, it's important to consider potential errors that may occur. This is where exception handling comes in. In this chapter, we will cover how to handle exceptions in Java and debugging techniques.

SUBCHAPTER 3.1: HANDLING EXCEPTIONS IN JAVA

Exceptions occur when unexpected situations arise during code execution. Java provides a mechanism to handle these situations without causing a program to crash. To handle exceptions, the try-catch block is used. The try block contains the code that may throw an exception, while the catch block catches and handles the exception. Java has several built-in exception classes, such as NullPointerException,

ArithmeticException, and IOException. It's important to understand the different types of exceptions to properly handle them in code. In addition to the try-catch block, Java also provides the finally block. This block is executed regardless of whether an exception is thrown or not. It's commonly used for releasing resources like files, database connections, or network sockets.

SUBCHAPTER 3.2: DEBUGGING TECHNIQUES AND TOOLS

Debugging is the process of finding and fixing errors in code. There are several techniques you can use to debug Java code, including print statements, logging, and debugging tools. Print statements are a quick and easy way to debug your code. By adding print statements in strategic locations, you can see the values of variables and the flow of your program. Logging is another useful technique for debugging. Java has a built-in logging framework, java.util.logging, that allows you to log messages at different levels, such as INFO, WARNING, and SEVERE. These logs can then be analyzed to identify issues in the code. Debugging tools such as Eclipse, NetBeans, and IntelliJ IDEA provide a more advanced way of debugging code. These tools allow you to step through your code line by line, set breakpoints, and inspect variables at runtime.

SUBCHAPTER 3.3: BEST PRACTICES FOR EXCEPTION HANDLING AND DEBUGGING

To effectively handle exceptions and debug code, it's important to follow best practices. Here are some tips to keep in mind: - Catch only the exceptions you're expecting and handle them appropriately. - Use meaningful error messages to provide insight into what went wrong. - Avoid catching generic exceptions like Exception or Throwable. - Use logging to track errors and debug potential issues. - Utilize debugging tools to help identify and fix problems. By following these best practices, you can ensure your code is robust and resilient to errors.

HANDLING EXCEPTIONS IN JAVA

Exception handling is a crucial part of developing robust and reliable Java applications. When an unexpected error occurs, it can cause your application to crash or produce incorrect results. In Java, exceptions are objects that represent errors or exceptional situations that occur during the runtime of a program. To handle exceptions in Java, you can use a try-catch block. The code that may throw an exception is enclosed in the try block, and the code to handle the exception is enclosed in the catch block. If an exception occurs in the try block, the catch block is executed. There are several types of exceptions in Java, including checked exceptions and unchecked exceptions. Checked exceptions are checked by the compiler at compile time and must be explicitly handled in the code. On the other hand, unchecked exceptions are not checked at compile time and can occur at runtime. It is important to handle exceptions appropriately to ensure that your application remains stable and reliable. You can also define your own exceptions by creating a new class that inherits from the Exception class. In summary, exception handling is crucial for developing reliable Java applications. You can use a try-catch block to handle exceptions, and there are different types of exceptions to be aware of. It is important to handle exceptions appropriately to ensure that your application remains stable and reliable.

SUBCHAPTER 3.2: DEBUGGING TECHNIQUES AND TOOLS

Debugging is an important aspect of software development, and Java provides developers with various tools and techniques to identify and fix bugs in their code. In this section, we will discuss some of the common debugging techniques and tools that are available to Java developers. One of the most common ways to debug Java code is by using breakpoints. A breakpoint is a point in your code where you want the program to stop executing so that you can inspect the values of specific variables, objects, or other data structures at that point in time. The Eclipse IDE provides an easy-to-use debugger that allows you to set breakpoints and step through your code line by line to identify any issues. Another useful debugging tool is the Java Virtual Machine (JVM) Debugger Interface (JDWP). JDWP is a protocol that allows debugging tools to communicate with a running JVM, enabling you to perform remote debugging on a Java program. This is especially useful if you are debugging a program that is running on a remote server. Logging is another technique that is commonly used to debug Java programs. Logging is the practice of generating log messages at various points in your code to record the flow of execution and identify any issues in the program. The Java Logging API provides developers with a powerful logging system that allows them to customize the level of granularity of their logs and filter them based on specific criteria. In addition, Java developers can also use various profiling tools to identify performance issues in their code. Profiling tools enable you to monitor the memory usage, CPU utilization, and other system metrics of your Java program, which can help you to optimize your code and improve its performance. Overall, debugging is an essential part of software development, and Java provides developers with an array of useful tools and techniques to identify and fix bugs in their code. By using the right tools and techniques, you can ensure that your Java programs are robust, efficient, and error-free.

BEST PRACTICES FOR EXCEPTION HANDLING AND DEBUGGING

Exception handling and debugging are two critical aspects of software development in Java. In this subchapter, we will discuss some best practices for effectively handling exceptions and debugging your Java applications. 1. Always use try-catch blocks: When writing Java code, it is important to always use try-catch blocks to catch any exceptions that may occur during runtime. This will help prevent your program from crashing and make it more robust. 2. Handle exceptions in the appropriate layer: Exceptions should be handled in the layer where they occur, rather than being passed up to a higher layer. This will make it easier to identify and resolve issues in your code. 3. Use custom exception classes: When creating your own exceptions, always create a custom exception class that extends the

Exception or RuntimeException class. This will make it easier to identify and handle specific types of exceptions in your code. 4. Log exceptions: It is important to log any exceptions that occur in your code to help identify and debug issues. Use a logging framework like Log4j or the Java Logging API to log exceptions. 5. Use debugging tools: Java provides a number of useful debugging tools like the Eclipse debugger or the jdb command-line debugger. Use these tools to step through your code, set breakpoints, and identify issues. 6. Write unit tests: Unit tests are a great way to identify and prevent issues in your code before they occur. Write unit tests that cover all possible scenarios and edge cases to ensure your code is working as intended. By following these best practices, you can ensure your Java applications are robust, reliable, and easy to debug.

Chapter 4: Java Collections Framework

Java collections framework is the core concept of Java programming language, which allows storing, manipulating, and processing a group of objects. This chapter will cover the fundamental concepts of collections framework, including Lists, Sets, and Maps, Iterators, and Generics.

SUBCHAPTER 4.1: LISTS, SETS, AND MAPS

Lists, Sets, and Maps are the three interfaces of the Java collections framework. A list is an ordered collection that allows duplicates, whereas a set is an unordered collection that does not allow any duplicates. A map is also an unordered collection that maps keys to values, and keys cannot be duplicated. In addition to these basic data structures, the Java collections framework provides several other data structures with advanced features such as Stack, Queue, and Deque.

SUBCHAPTER 4.2: ITERATORS AND GENERICS

Iterators are a way to traverse the elements of a collection one by one. It allows the developer to access each element of the collection without knowing the underlying structure of the collection. The Java collections framework provides three types of iterators, including Fail Fast, Fail Safe, and Enumeration. Generics are a way of parameterizing data types. It allows developers to declare the data type of the elements in the collection at the time of creating the collection. Generics provide type safety, which means that the compiler ensures the type of objects inserted into the collection matches the declared type.

SUBCHAPTER 4.3: SORTING AND SEARCHING TECHNIQUES

Sorting and Searching are two of the most common algorithms used for manipulating collections. The Java collections framework provides several algorithms for sorting, including Bubble Sort, Insertion Sort, Selection Sort, Quick Sort, and Merge Sort. Searching techniques include Linear Search, Binary Search, Interpolation search, and Jump search. Each search algorithm has its own advantages and disadvantages based on the data set being searched. In conclusion, mastering the concepts of Lists, Sets, and Maps, Iterators, and Generics, and Sorting and Searching algorithms will enable Java developers to build efficient and effective applications using the collections framework.

LISTS, SETS, AND MAPS

Java Collections Framework provides three main data structures known as Lists, Sets, and Maps. These data structures help programmers to organize and manage their data more efficiently while also providing various useful functionalities. **Lists:** Lists are ordered collections of elements that allow duplicates, and are indexed starting from 0. Java provides two main list implementations: ArrayList and LinkedList. ArrayList is a resizable array that provides fast random access times, while LinkedList provides better performance for adding and removing elements despite slower random access times. **Sets:** Sets are unordered collections of unique elements that do not allow duplicates. Java provides three main set implementations: HashSet, LinkedHashSet, and TreeSet. HashSet provides the fastest performance for adding and removing elements, but does not maintain order.

LinkedHashSet maintains the order of insertion, while TreeSet sorts elements based on their natural order. **Maps:** Maps are collections of key-value pairs, where each key is unique and is used to retrieve its corresponding value. Java provides several map implementations, including HashMap, LinkedHashMap, and TreeMap. HashMap provides constant-time performance for basic operations such as adding, removing, and retrieving values based on the keys. LinkedHashMap maintains order and HashMap properties, while TreeMap sorts key-value pairs based on either their natural order or a comparator. Understanding these data structures and their characteristics is crucial for designing efficient and reliable applications. In the next subchapter, we will dive deeper into the functionalities of these data structures, and explore how to effectively utilize them in Java programming.

ITERATORS AND GENERICS

When working with collections in Java, Iterators are essential tools. They allow us to traverse and manipulate collections in a safe, efficient, and standardized way. An iterator is an interface that provides methods to retrieve, remove and check whether the collection has more elements. Generics, on the other hand, provide a way to make collections type-safe by specifying the type of elements that a collection can contain. This allows us to write code that is more robust, more readable, and less error-prone. The Iterator interface provides three fundamental methods: hasNext(), next(), and remove(). The hasNext() method returns true if there are more elements in the collection, next() returns the next element, and remove() removes the last element returned by next(). Generics allow us to specify the type of elements that a collection can contain, making our code more type-safe and less error-prone. Before Java 5, Collection classes were not generic, and we had to cast the elements in a collection before using them. Generics allow us to eliminate castings and check at compile time whether we are dealing with the correct type of objects. An example of using a generic Iterator could be: MSONormal List names = new ArrayList<>(); names.add("John"); names.add("Mary"); names.add("Bob"); Iterator iterator = names.iterator(); while(iterator.hasNext()) { System.out.println(iterator.next()); } The code above creates a List of strings, adds some names to it, and then creates an Iterator that is used to print out each name in the list. The Iterator is type-safe because we have specified the type of elements it can retrieve in the Iterator's generic. In summary, Iterators and Generics are fundamental components of the Java Collections Framework. They make our code more robust, efficient, and type-safe. By using Generics, we can avoid potential type casting errors at compile-time, and using Iterators allows us to safely iterate through collections while manipulating them.

SUBCHAPTER 4.3: SORTING AND SEARCHING TECHNIQUES

Sorting and searching are fundamental operations in any programming language and Java is no exception. In this section, we will cover various sorting and searching techniques that are widely used in Java.

Sorting Techniques

Java provides several built-in sorting algorithms that can be used to sort arrays or collections. Let's take a look at some of the most commonly used sorting algorithms in Java. **Bubble Sort:** Bubble sort is one of the simplest sorting algorithms. It repeatedly passes through the array and swaps adjacent elements if they are in the wrong order. **Selection Sort:** Selection sort repeatedly selects the smallest element from the unsorted part of the array and places it at the beginning. **Insertion Sort:** Insertion sort inserts elements from unsorted part to the sorted part of the array one by one. **Merge Sort:** Merge sort is a divide and conquer algorithm that divides the array into smaller arrays, sorts them and then merges them back together. **Quick Sort:** Quick sort is also a divide and conquer algorithm where a pivot element is selected and the array is partitioned into two sub-arrays such that elements smaller than pivot are on one side and elements greater than pivot are on the other side. The process is recursively applied to the two sub-arrays.

Searching Techniques

Java provides several built-in searching algorithms that can be used to search arrays or collections. Let's take a look at some of the most commonly used searching algorithms in Java. **Linear Search:** Linear search is the simplest search algorithm. It searches the element in the array or collection by comparing it with each element sequentially. **Binary Search:**

Binary search is a more efficient searching algorithm when the array or collection is sorted. It works by repeatedly dividing the search interval in half until the element is found or the search interval is empty.
Hashing: Hashing is a technique for storing and retrieving data quickly. It works by using a hash function to generate a unique key for each item in the collection. The key is used to look up the item in a hash table. These sorting and searching techniques are essential for developing efficient and optimized Java applications. It is important to choose the appropriate algorithm based on the size of the data set and the desired efficiency. In the next section, we will cover multithreading and concurrency techniques in Java.

Chapter 5: Multithreading and Concurrency

Multithreading and concurrency are essential concepts for developing robust and efficient Java programs. This chapter explores how to use threads and processes for parallel computation and how to synchronize them to prevent race conditions and deadlocks.

SUBCHAPTER 5.1: THREADS AND PROCESSES IN JAVA

In Java, a thread is a lightweight and independent unit of execution that can run concurrently with other threads in the same program. A process, on the other hand, is a complete program execution environment that includes multiple threads and their associated resources. Creating a new thread in Java involves either extending the Thread class or implementing the Runnable interface. The former approach is known as a subclassing thread, while the latter is known as a worker thread. Both approaches allow you to define the code to be executed in the new thread's run method. Java provides several methods for managing threads, including starting, pausing, resuming, and stopping them. However, you should always use these methods with caution and follow best practices for thread safety and synchronization.

SUBCHAPTER 5.2: THREAD SYNCHRONIZATION MECHANISMS

Synchronization is the process of coordinating the execution of multiple threads to ensure that they access shared resources in a mutually exclusive and predictable manner. In Java, synchronization is achieved through various mechanisms, including locks, monitors, semaphores, and barriers. Locks are the most basic form of synchronization and control access to a shared resource through the use of a mutual exclusion flag. Monitors enhance locks by adding a wait/notify mechanism that enables threads to block and awake on specific conditions. Semaphores provide a more flexible synchronization mechanism by allowing threads to wait and signal on arbitrary integer values. Barriers enable multiple threads to synchronize at specific points in a program by waiting for each other to reach a designated point.

SUBCHAPTER 5.3: CONCURRENT PROGRAMMING BEST PRACTICES

Writing efficient and scalable concurrent programs requires following several best practices, including minimizing contention, minimizing synchronization scope, using immutable data structures, using thread-safe collections, and avoiding thread dependencies. Minimizing contention involves reducing the number of threads that need to access the same shared resource simultaneously. This can be achieved by partitioning data, creating private copies, or using non-blocking algorithms. Minimizing synchronization scope involves limiting the regions of code that require synchronization to avoid holding locks longer than necessary. This can be achieved by moving synchronization blocks to specific methods or classes and avoiding nested locks. Using immutable data structures involves creating objects that cannot be modified once created, which eliminates the possibility of data inconsistency in multi-threaded environments. Thread-safe collections are collections that are specifically designed to be used concurrently, such as ConcurrentHashMap and CopyOnWriteArrayList. Avoiding thread dependencies involves designing programs such that thread safety is an inherent property of the architecture. This can be achieved by isolating mutable state and by minimizing inter-thread communication.

THREADS AND PROCESSES IN JAVA

Java is a multi-threaded programming language, meaning that a single program can execute multiple threads of code concurrently. This allows for greater efficiency and responsiveness in applications. In Java, threads are created and controlled using the Thread class. Each thread has its own call stack and can execute its own code independently from other threads. Processes, on the other hand, are separate instances of a program running in their own memory space. Java also provides a mechanism for inter-thread communication and synchronization through the use of locks, conditions, and semaphores. This allows for coordination between threads and prevents conflicts when accessing shared resources. Understanding how threads and processes work in Java is essential for developing efficient and scalable applications. In the next subchapter, we will dive deeper into thread synchronization mechanisms.

THREAD SYNCHRONIZATION MECHANISMS

In Java, when multiple threads are working with shared resources, it is essential to synchronize their operations to avoid inconsistencies and unexpected behavior. Thread synchronization mechanisms help ensure that one thread completes its operation before another thread starts with the same resource. One way to achieve synchronization is by using the **synchronized** keyword. This keyword can be used with a block of code, or a method, or a static method. The synchronized keyword maintains a lock on the current object or on a specified object. Only one thread can acquire the lock at a time, and other threads that attempt to access the resource wait for the lock to be released. Another way to achieve synchronization is by using **semaphores**. A semaphore is a control structure that allows threads to access shared resources in a mutually exclusive manner. A semaphore has a set of permits that represent the number of threads that can access the shared resource at a time. Java also provides **monitors** that help synchronize threads. A monitor is a high-level synchronization mechanism that can be used to protect shared resources.

Monitors rely on the wait() and notify() methods. The wait() method is used to wait for a specific condition to occur, while the notify() method is used to signal that the condition has occurred. Finally, there are **locks**. Locks provide a way to lock a specific block of code and ensure that only one thread can execute that block of code at a time. A lock can be used to protect multiple resources and can be more flexible than the synchronized keyword. Thread synchronization mechanisms are critical in Java programming and must be used to avoid race conditions and ensure consistent behavior. Choosing the right synchronization mechanism depends on the specific use case and the shared resource in question.

CONCURRENT PROGRAMMING BEST PRACTICES

Concurrency is the ability to run multiple tasks simultaneously. It is a crucial part of modern software development, and mastering it can make all the difference when it comes to designing high-performance applications. In this subchapter, we will explore some of the best practices for concurrent programming in Java. These practices will help you avoid common pitfalls and ensure that your multi-threaded applications are robust and performant.

1. Avoid Shared Mutable State

Sharing mutable state between threads is one of the most common sources of bugs in concurrent programming. Mutable state refers to any data that can be modified after it has been initialized. If this state is shared between threads, then it can lead to race conditions, deadlocks, and other synchronization issues. To avoid these problems, you should try to minimize the amount of shared mutable state in your programs. Instead, use immutable objects or thread-safe data structures wherever possible. If you do need to share mutable state, then you should use synchronized methods or locks to control access to that state.

2. Keep Critical Sections Small

A critical section is a portion of code that must be executed atomically. That is, it must be executed by a single thread at a time to ensure correctness. However, if you make critical sections too large, then you can create contention between threads, leading to poor performance. To avoid this problem, you should try to keep your critical sections as small as possible. This means minimizing the amount of code that needs to be executed atomically and releasing locks as soon as possible.

3. Use Thread Pools

Creating and destroying threads can be an expensive process. If you need to perform multiple short-lived tasks, then creating a new thread for each task can slow down your application significantly. To avoid this problem, you should use thread pools. A thread pool is a group of pre-allocated threads that are ready to execute tasks as they become available. By reusing threads, you can avoid the overhead of creating and destroying threads and improve the overall performance of your application.

4. Use Atomic Variables and Synchronization Primitives

When working with shared mutable state, it's important to use appropriate synchronization primitives to ensure that the state remains consistent across threads. One common primitive is the atomic variable. An atomic variable is a variable that can be updated atomically, without the need for locks or other synchronization mechanisms. This makes it a useful tool for updating shared state in a multi-threaded environment.

5. Test Your Code Thoroughly

Finally, when writing concurrent programs, it's important to test your code thoroughly.

Multi-threaded programs can be challenging to debug, and even small bugs can be difficult to track down. One effective approach is to use stress testing. Stress testing involves subjecting your program to a large number of concurrent users or tasks and monitoring its performance and behavior. This can help you identify bottlenecks and other issues before they become serious problems in production. By following these best practices, you can write robust, performant, and reliable concurrent programs in Java.## Working with Files and Databases In this chapter, we will explore how to work with files and databases in Java. In today's technology-driven world, data storage and retrieval have become essential parts of software development. We will cover essential topics such as file input-output operations, Java Database Connectivity (JDBC) programming, and Object-Relational Mapping with Hibernate. ### File Input-Output Operations in Java Java provides built-in libraries for input-output operations with files. Whether you need to read data from a file or write data to a file, there are many classes available to handle these tasks. In this section, we will explore these classes and their methods in detail.

JDBC Programming and Database Integration

JDBC programming is a standard that defines how a Java application interacts with relational databases. With JDBC, you can connect to a database, execute SQL statements, and retrieve results. In this section, we will see how JDBC works and how to use it to communicate with databases in Java.

Object-Relational Mapping with Hibernate

Hibernate is a popular Object-Relational Mapping (ORM) tool that provides a framework for mapping Java objects to relational databases. It eliminates the need for boiler-plate code and simplifies the database integration process. In this section, we will learn about Hibernate's features, how to set up the configuration, and how to perform basic database operations using Hibernate. By the end of this chapter, you will have a solid understanding of file input-output operations, JDBC programming, and Object-Relational Mapping with Hibernate. You will be able to store and retrieve data files and databases in Java applications. Let's dive in!

SUBCHAPTER 6.1: FILE INPUT-OUTPUT OPERATIONS IN JAVA

Java provides several classes for performing input-output operations on files. In this subchapter, we will discuss the basics of file input-output operations in Java. Java's **java.io.File** class is used for creating, deleting, and renaming files and directories. The File class provides several useful method for manipulating files and directories, such as **createNewFile()**, **delete()**, **renameTo()**, and **list()**. To read data from a file, Java provides several classes such as **FileInputStream**, **FileReader**, and **BufferedReader**. Similarly, to write data to a file, Java provides classes such as **FileOutputStream**, **FileWriter**, and

BufferedWriter. The **FileInputStream** and **FileOutputStream** classes are used for reading and writing binary data, while **FileReader** and **FileWriter** classes are used for reading and writing character data. Here is an example of reading data from a file using the **FileReader** and **BufferedReader** classes:

```
File file = new File("data.txt");

try (FileReader fileReader = new
FileReader(file);
     BufferedReader bufferedReader = new
BufferedReader(fileReader)) {

    String line;
    while ((line = bufferedReader.readLine())
!= null) {
        System.out.println(line);
    }
} catch (IOException e) {
    e.printStackTrace();
}
```

In this example, we first create a **File** object for the file we want to read. Then we create a **FileReader** and a **BufferedReader** object and pass them the **File** object. After that, we read the file line by line using the **readLine()** method of the **BufferedReader** object and print each line to the console. To write data to a file, we can use similar classes and methods. Here is an example of writing data to a file using the **FileWriter** and **BufferedWriter** classes:

```
try (FileWriter fileWriter = new FileWriter("data.txt");
     BufferedWriter bufferedWriter = new BufferedWriter(fileWriter)) {

    bufferedWriter.write("Hello, World!");
    bufferedWriter.newLine();
    bufferedWriter.write("This is a new line.");

} catch (IOException e) {
    e.printStackTrace();
}
```

In this example, we first create a **FileWriter** and a **BufferedWriter** object for the file we want to write. Then we use the **write()** method of the **BufferedWriter** object to write data to the file. We also use the **newLine()** method of the **BufferedWriter** object to add a newline character after each line. In conclusion, Java provides powerful classes and methods for performing file input-output operations. By using the appropriate classes and methods, you can easily read and write data from and to files in your Java programs.

SUBCHAPTER 6.2: JDBC PROGRAMMING AND DATABASE INTEGRATION

Java Database Connectivity (JDBC) is a standard that defines how Java applications connect to and interact with databases. JDBC programming allows Java developers to write code that can dynamically interact with various databases. In this subchapter, we will explore the basics of JDBC programming and how to integrate databases into Java applications.

Connecting to a Database

To connect to a database using JDBC, we need to obtain a database connection. The `java.sql.Connection` interface is used to establish a connection to the database. To obtain a connection, we first need to load a database driver. This is done using the `Class.forName()` method, which loads the driver class into memory. Once the driver is loaded, we can use the `DriverManager` class to get a connection to the database. The `DriverManager.getConnection()` method is used to establish a database connection. Here's an example:

```
import java.sql.*;
public class DatabaseExample {
    public static void main(String[] args) {
        Connection conn = null;
        try {
            Class.forName("com.mysql.jdbc.Driver");
            conn = DriverManager.getConnection("jdbc:mysql://localhost:3306/mydatabase", "username", "password");
            System.out.println("Connected to the database");
        } catch (Exception e) {
            e.printStackTrace();
        } finally {
            if (conn != null) {
                try {
                    conn.close();
                } catch (SQLException e) {
                    e.printStackTrace();
                }
            }
        }
    }
}
```

In this example, we're using the MySQL database and the `com.mysql.jdbc.Driver` driver class. We're also providing the database URL, username, and password to the `DriverManager.getConnection()` method.

Executing SQL Statements

Once we have a database connection, we can execute SQL statements using the `java.sql.Statement` interface. The `Statement` interface provides methods for executing SQL queries and updates. Here's an example of how to execute a simple SQL query: ``` import java.sql.*; public class DatabaseExample { public static void main(String[] args) { Connection conn = null; Statement stmt = null; ResultSet rs = null; try { Class.forName("com.mysql.jdbc.Driver"); conn = DriverManager.getConnection("jdbc:mysql://localhost:3306/mydatabase", "username", "password"); stmt = conn.createStatement(); rs = stmt.executeQuery("SELECT * FROM mytable"); while (rs.next()) { int id = rs.getInt("id"); String name = rs.getString("name"); System.out.println("ID: " + id + ", Name: " + name); } } catch (Exception e) { e.printStackTrace(); } finally { if (rs != null) { try { rs.close(); } catch (SQLException e)

{ e.printStackTrace(); } } if (stmt != null) { try { stmt.close(); } catch (SQLException e) { e.printStackTrace(); } } if (conn != null) { try { conn.close(); } catch (SQLException e) { e.printStackTrace(); } } } } ``` In this example, we're executing a SQL query to select all records from a table named `mytable`. We're then iterating over the results using a `ResultSet` object and printing the values of each row.

Using Prepared Statements

To prevent SQL injection attacks and improve performance, it's recommended to use prepared statements instead of simple SQL statements for executing queries with dynamic parameters. A prepared statement is a SQL statement that is first parsed and compiled by the database. Then, it can be executed multiple times with different parameters. Here's an example of how to use a prepared statement: ``` import java.sql.*; public class DatabaseExample { public static void main(String[] args) { Connection conn = null; PreparedStatement stmt = null; ResultSet rs = null; try { Class.forName("com.mysql.jdbc.Driver"); conn = DriverManager.getConnection("jdbc:mysql://localhost:3306/mydatabase", "username", "password"); stmt = conn.prepareStatement("SELECT * FROM mytable WHERE id = ?"); stmt.setInt(1, 1); rs = stmt.executeQuery(); while (rs.next()) { int id = rs.getInt("id"); String name = rs.getString("name"); System.out.println("ID: " + id + ", Name: " + name); } } catch (Exception e) { e.printStackTrace(); } finally { if (rs != null) { try { rs.close(); } catch (SQLException e) { e.printStackTrace(); } } if (stmt != null) { try { stmt.close(); } catch (SQLException e) { e.printStackTrace(); } } if (conn != null) { try { conn.close(); } catch (SQLException e) { e.printStackTrace(); } } } } ``` In this example, we're using a prepared statement to select a record from the `mytable` table with an `id` of 1. We're then iterating over the results using a `ResultSet` object and printing the values of each row.

Conclusion

JDBC programming is an important skill for Java developers who need to integrate databases into their applications. In this subchapter, we covered the basics of connecting to and interacting with databases using JDBC. Remember to always use prepared statements for executing queries with dynamic parameters to prevent SQL injection attacks and improve performance.

OBJECT-RELATIONAL MAPPING WITH HIBERNATE

Hibernate is an open-source, lightweight, and powerful ORM (Object-Relational Mapping) tool for Java. It provides a framework for mapping an object-oriented domain model to a relational database. Hibernate allows developers to work with objects in their Java code without having to worry about the persistent storage or retrieval of data. With Hibernate, developers can create Domain Objects

(POJOs) and map them to the database tables. Hibernate provides a simple configuration file and a set of annotations to map the domain objects to database tables. This makes it easy to switch between different database providers without needing to change the code. Hibernate supports a wide range of database providers such as Oracle, MySQL, Microsoft SQL Server, and PostgreSQL. Hibernate also provides support for transaction handling, caching, and lazy loading. This makes it a very powerful tool for developing enterprise-level applications. With Hibernate, developers can write a single set of Java code that can be translated into SQL by Hibernate. This allows for clean and easy-to-understand code, as there is no need for cumbersome SQL statements. Developers can concentrate on writing clean Java code and let Hibernate handle the database interactions. Furthermore, Hibernate makes it easy to handle complex relationships between Domain Objects. Hibernate automatically creates the necessary JOIN statements to make this work. This means that developers can focus on creating the business logic in their Java code and let Hibernate handle the database queries. In summary, Hibernate is a powerful and easy-to-use ORM tool for Java developers. It provides a simple way to map Domain Objects to a database and handle complex relationships between them. Hibernate allows developers to write clean Java code without the need for cumbersome SQL statements. Hibernate is an essential tool for developers looking to create enterprise-level applications.

Chapter 7: Java Networking and Security

Java is widely used for developing network-based applications. In this chapter, we will discuss the basic concepts of network programming in Java and cover some important aspects of Java security.

SUBCHAPTER 7.1: SOCKET PROGRAMMING IN JAVA

Java provides robust support for developing network-based applications through the use of sockets. Sockets are endpoints for communication between two machines in a network. In Java, we can use the `Socket` and `ServerSocket` classes provided by the `java.net` package to create sockets. The `Socket` class represents a client-side socket, while the `ServerSocket` class represents a server-side socket. Using sockets, we can establish a connection between a client and a server and send and receive data between them. Networking programming in Java involves handling exceptions, multi-threading, and encoding/decoding of data.

Handling Exceptions in Networking

Network programming in Java involves handling various exceptions that can occur during the communication process. Some of the common exceptions include `UnknownHostException`, `IOException`, `SocketTimeoutException`, and `SocketException`. It is important to handle these exceptions gracefully to avoid application crashes and ensure the robustness of the application.

Multi-threading in Networking

Multi-threading is a critical aspect of network programming in Java. Sockets can block until a communication is complete, which can lead to delays in the application. By handling sockets in separate threads, we can avoid these delays and ensure the smooth functioning of the application.

Encoding/Decoding Data in Networking

In Java, data is sent as bytes over the network. However, the sender and receiver of the data may have different character encodings. It is important to ensure that the data is encoded and decoded properly to avoid data corruption or loss during the communication process.

SUBCHAPTER 7.2: SECURING JAVA APPLICATIONS WITH CRYPTOGRAPHY

Java provides built-in support for cryptography through the `javax.crypto` package. Cryptography is used to provide secure communication and data transfer over the network. The `javax.crypto` package provides various classes and interfaces for encryption and decryption, key generation, and secure random number generation. Java also supports various cryptographic algorithms, such as AES,

RSA, and SHA, among others. The key concepts of cryptography include confidentiality, integrity, and authentication. Confidentiality ensures that sensitive information is kept secret and cannot be accessed by unauthorized parties. Integrity ensures that the data cannot be tampered with during the communication process. Authentication ensures that the parties involved in the communication are who they claim to be.

Best Practices for Java Security

Securing Java applications involves following certain best practices, such as using strong passwords, keeping the software up-to-date, restricting access to sensitive information, and using encryption for sensitive data. It is also important to use third-party libraries and frameworks that have been security tested and avoid using deprecated or vulnerable APIs. Regular security audits are necessary to ensure the security of the application.

SOCKET PROGRAMMING IN JAVA

In today's interconnected world, networking has become an essential part of software development. Socket programming is a powerful tool for creating networked applications in Java, and is used extensively in web servers, chat applications, and other distributed systems. At its core, socket programming involves the use of "sockets", which are endpoints for communication between two devices over a network. In Java, this is accomplished through the use of the java.net package, which provides classes for implementing network protocols. One of the main advantages of socket programming is its versatility. Sockets can be used to create both client and server applications, and can support a variety of communication protocols, including TCP and UDP. When implementing socket programming in Java, it is important to consider issues such as error handling, data serialization, and security. Best practices include using separate threads for networking operations, carefully validating user input to prevent security vulnerabilities, and using encryption to protect sensitive data. In the following chapters, we will explore more advanced socket programming topics, including network security and server scalability. With the help of Java's powerful networking libraries, the possibilities for creating powerful and flexible networked applications are virtually limitless.

SECURING JAVA APPLICATIONS WITH CRYPTOGRAPHY

Cryptography is the science of secure communication in the presence of third parties. Java provides strong support for cryptography and enables developers to secure their applications using various encryption and decryption techniques. One of the most commonly used cryptographic techniques in Java is the Advanced Encryption Standard (AES). This algorithm provides strong encryption and decryption capabilities and is commonly used to secure sensitive data in Java applications. Another important cryptographic technique used in Java is the Digital Signature Algorithm (DSA). This algorithm allows developers to generate and verify digital signatures, which can be used to ensure the authenticity and integrity of data. Java also provides support for various key management techniques, such as key pairs, key stores, and key chains. These techniques enable developers to securely store and manage their encryption keys, which are crucial for ensuring the security of their applications. It's important to note that while cryptography can be a powerful tool for securing Java applications, it's not a silver bullet. Developers must also implement other security measures, such as input validation and access control, to ensure the overall security of their applications. In summary, cryptography is an essential component of Java application security, and developers must be familiar with various encryption and decryption techniques to secure their applications. Additionally, developers must also implement other security measures to ensure the overall security of their applications.

BEST PRACTICES FOR JAVA SECURITY

Java is one of the most popular programming languages in the world, and as such, is targeted by many cybercriminals looking to exploit vulnerabilities in Java applications. Therefore, it is important to follow best practices when it comes to Java security. Here are some key tips to help you keep your Java applications secure:

1. Keep Java Updated

One of the easiest ways to improve Java security is to keep your Java installation updated. Oracle frequently releases patches and updates to Java that include important security fixes. Ensure that you regularly install these updates to keep your Java environment secure.

2. Use Secure Coding Practices

Developers should take care to follow secure coding practices when developing Java applications. This includes avoiding hardcoding sensitive information like passwords and using secure authentication mechanisms instead. Additionally, ensure that you check all input from users to avoid vulnerabilities like SQL injection.

3. Use Encryption for Sensitive Data

Sensitive information like passwords and credit card numbers should be encrypted in your Java applications. This helps to ensure that if an attacker gains access to your data, they will not be able to read it.

4. Limit Access to Sensitive Resources

Access to sensitive resources like files and databases should be limited to only those who need it. For example, if you have a database containing sensitive customer information, only specific employees should be allowed to access that data.

5. Implement Access Controls

Access controls should be implemented to limit what users can do in your Java application. This includes restricting access to certain functions and data based on user roles and permissions.

6. Use SSL/TLS for Network Communications

If your Java application communicates with other applications or services over a network, ensure that you use SSL/TLS to encrypt that communication. This helps to prevent attackers from intercepting or modifying data in transit.

7. Regularly Conduct Security Audits

Regularly auditing the security of your Java application can help you identify potential vulnerabilities before they are exploited. This includes penetration testing and code reviews. By following these best practices, you can help to ensure that your Java applications are secure and protected from potential cyber threats.

Chapter 8: Java Web Development

Web development with Java is a powerful and widely used technology for creating dynamic and interactive web applications. In this chapter, we will cover the fundamentals of Java web development, including the basics of web technologies, servlets, JSP programming, and web services with RESTful APIs.

INTRODUCTION TO WEB TECHNOLOGIES

Web technologies are the building blocks of the internet. In Java web development, we use a combination of front-end and back-end technologies to create dynamic and responsive web applications. Some of the most common web technologies used in Java web development include:

HTML and CSS:

HTML is a markup language that is used to structure and format content on the web. CSS is a styling language that is used to control the appearance of HTML elements.

JavaScript:

JavaScript is a scripting language that is used to add interactivity and dynamic functionality to web pages.

Servlets and JSP Programming:

Servlets are server-side Java programs that run on a web server and handle client requests. JSP (JavaServer Pages) is a technology that is used to create dynamic web pages using Java.

Web Services:

Web services are APIs (Application Programming Interfaces) that are exposed over the web. Clients can use web services to interact with your application and retrieve data.

SERVLETS AND JSP PROGRAMMING

Servlets are a fundamental part of Java web development. They are used to handle client requests and generate dynamic content. A servlet is a Java program that extends the javax.servlet.Servlet interface and runs on a web server. When a client sends a request to a servlet, the servlet generates a response and sends it back to the client. JSP (JavaServer Pages) is a technology that is used to create dynamic web pages using Java. JSP pages are compiled on the server side and generate HTML content that is sent to the client. JSP pages are similar to HTML pages, but they also include Java code that is executed on the server side.

WEB SERVICES WITH RESTFUL APIS

REST (Representational State Transfer) is a web architecture that is used to create lightweight, scalable web services. RESTful APIs are a type of web service that follows the REST architecture. They are flexible, easy to use, and can be consumed by a wide range of clients, including web browsers, mobile devices, and other applications. In RESTful API development, resources are identified by URLs (Uniform Resource Locators). Clients can interact with these resources using HTTP methods, such as GET, POST, PUT, and DELETE. RESTful

APIs typically return data in JSON (JavaScript Object Notation) or XML (Extensible Markup Language) format. Overall, Java web development is a powerful and flexible technology for building dynamic and interactive web applications. By leveraging the power of servlets, JSP programming, and RESTful APIs, you can create scalable and responsive web applications that meet the needs of your users.

INTRODUCTION TO WEB TECHNOLOGIES

Web technologies have revolutionized the way we interact with the internet and have opened up a whole new world of possibilities. Some of the most popular web technologies include HTML, CSS, JavaScript, and AJAX. HTML (Hypertext Markup Language) is the foundation of web development and is used to create the structure and content of web pages. CSS (Cascading Style Sheets) is used for styling

HTML documents and making them visually appealing. JavaScript is used for creating dynamic and interactive web pages that can respond to user actions. AJAX (Asynchronous JavaScript And XML) is used for creating web applications that can fetch and send data to web servers without requiring a page refresh. In order to become a successful web developer, you will need to familiarize yourself with these key technologies as well as other web development frameworks and tools. Understanding the basics of web technologies is the first step to building robust web applications that can provide a seamless user experience. In the following chapters, we will cover the main web development technologies in depth and explore how they can be used to create modern web applications.

SERVLETS AND JSP PROGRAMMING

When it comes to developing dynamic web applications, Servlets and JSP (JavaServer Pages) are the two most essential Java technologies. A Servlet is a Java class that is used to handle the HTTP requests and generate dynamic web pages, while JSP is a technology used to create HTML pages with embedded Java code. Servlets provide a way to extend the capabilities of a web server, allowing you to handle dynamic content creation, security, and session management. They can be used to process form data, generate dynamic content, and perform other server-side tasks. JSP pages are similar to regular HTML pages but include special tags that are used to embed Java code within the HTML. This allows you to create dynamic web pages that can change based on user input or other variables. One of the main benefits of using Servlets and JSP is that they are platform-independent, meaning that they can run on any platform that supports Java. Additionally, they provide a scalable and efficient way to handle web traffic and can help to improve the performance of your web applications. To get started with Servlets and JSP programming, you will need to set up a web server such as Apache Tomcat or Jetty, and then create your Servlets and JSP pages using a Java IDE such as Eclipse or IntelliJ IDEA. There are many resources available online to help you learn more about Servlets and JSP, including tutorials, books, and online courses. With practice and dedication, you can master these technologies and create dynamic, interactive web applications with ease.

SUBCHAPTER 8.3: WEB SERVICES WITH RESTFUL APIS

RESTful APIs (Application Programming Interfaces) have become the de facto standard for implementing web services due to their simplicity and flexibility. In this subchapter, we will delve into the key principles of RESTful web services and explore how they can be implemented using Java. At its core, REST is an architectural style that provides a set of guidelines for creating stateless, lightweight, and scalable web services. RESTful APIs use HTTP methods such as GET, POST, PUT, DELETE, and PATCH to operate on resources identified by URIs (Uniform Resource Identifiers). One of the key advantages of RESTful APIs is their ability to support multiple data formats, including JSON, XML, and YAML. This makes it easier for clients to consume the APIs and for developers to build loosely coupled systems that can evolve independently. To implement RESTful web services in Java, we can use a number of frameworks, including Spring Boot, JAX-RS, and Jersey. These frameworks facilitate the creation of RESTful endpoints and provide support for defining resource representations, handling request and response headers, and performing content negotiation. When designing a RESTful API, it's important to follow certain best practices to ensure scalability, maintainability, and ease of use. This includes defining meaningful and consistent resource URIs, adhering to HTTP conventions, enforcing input validation, and providing useful error messages. In conclusion, RESTful web services provide a powerful and flexible mechanism for integrating disparate systems and enabling seamless data exchange. By leveraging the principles of REST, developers can create robust and scalable APIs that are simple to use and easy to maintain. In the next chapter, we will explore the fundamental concepts of design patterns and their application in Java development.

Chapter 9: Design Patterns and Best Practices

SUBCHAPTER 9.1: GANG OF FOUR DESIGN PATTERNS

One of the most important aspects of developing software is being able to write code that is modular, extensible, and maintainable. Design patterns can help achieve these goals by providing proven solutions to common programming problems. The Gang of Four (GoF) is a group of four authors who wrote the book "Design Patterns: Elements of Reusable Object-Oriented Software". This book is widely regarded as the definitive resource on software design patterns. The authors of the book identified 23 design patterns that can be used to solve common programming problems. In this subchapter, we will explore some of the most commonly used design patterns, including the Singleton, Factory Method, and Observer patterns. We will also discuss how to apply these patterns in real-world scenarios.

The Singleton Pattern

The Singleton pattern is used when we want to ensure that only one instance of a class exists in the entire application. This can be useful in situations where there is a limited resource, such as a database connection, and we want to ensure that this resource is shared throughout the application. To implement the Singleton pattern in Java, we can create a class with a private constructor and a static method that returns an instance of the class. This method can check if an instance of the class has already been created, and if not, create a new instance.

The Factory Method Pattern

The Factory Method pattern is used when we want to create objects without specifying the exact class of object that will be created. This can be useful when we want to encapsulate the creation of objects and make it easier to change the implementation in the future. To implement the Factory Method pattern, we can create an interface or abstract class that defines a method for creating objects. Each concrete implementation of this interface or abstract class can create a different type of object.

The Observer Pattern

The Observer pattern is used when we want to notify multiple objects when a particular event occurs. This can be useful in situations where we want to decouple the producer of an event from the consumers that need to be notified. To implement the Observer pattern, we can create an interface that defines the methods that will be called when an event occurs. Each object that wants to be notified of the event can implement this interface and register with the object that produces the event.

SUBCHAPTER 9.2: ARCHITECTURAL PATTERNS AND BEST PRACTICES

In addition to design patterns, there are also architectural patterns that can be used to guide the overall structure and organization of a software system. These patterns can help ensure that the system is flexible, scalable, and maintainable. In this subchapter, we will explore some of the most commonly used architectural patterns, including the Model-View-Controller (MVC), Layered Architecture, and Microservices patterns. We will also discuss best practices for designing and implementing software systems.

The Model-View-Controller Pattern

The Model-View-Controller (MVC) pattern is used to separate the concerns of a software system into three distinct components: the Model, which represents the data and business logic of the system; the View, which represents the user interface; and the Controller, which handles user input and updates the Model and View accordingly. This separation of concerns can make it easier to maintain and modify the system, as changes to one component do not affect the others.

Layered Architecture

Layered Architecture is a pattern that divides a software system into layers, with each layer responsible for a specific set of functionality. This can help ensure that the system is modular, with each layer having a well-defined interface that can be used by other layers. A typical layered architecture includes a presentation layer, a business logic layer, and a data access layer.

Microservices

The Microservices architectural pattern is used to build large, complex systems by breaking them down into smaller, more manageable services. Each service performs a single, specific function and communicates with other services as needed. This can make it easier to develop, test, and deploy the system, as changes to one service do not affect the others. However, it also requires careful attention to the communication between services and the management of dependencies.

SUBCHAPTER 9.3: JAVA CODE REFACTORING TECHNIQUES

Refactoring is the process of improving the design of existing code without changing its external behavior. This can help make code more maintainable, extensible, and easier to understand. In this subchapter, we will explore some of the most commonly used refactoring techniques, including Extract Method, Extract Class, and Replace Conditional with Polymorphism.

Extract Method

The Extract Method refactoring technique is used to break a large method into smaller, more manageable pieces. This can make the code more readable and easier to understand, as well as making it easier to test and modify. To use the Extract Method technique, we can identify a block of code that performs a specific task and extract it into a separate method. We can then call this method from the original method, passing in any necessary parameters.

Extract Class

The Extract Class refactoring technique is used to move a set of related fields and methods from one class to a new class. This can make it easier to organize the code and reduce the complexity of the original class. To use the Extract Class technique, we can identify a set of fields and methods that are related and move them to a new class. We can then create a reference to the new class in the original class and update any code that references the old fields and methods.

Replace Conditional with Polymorphism

The Replace Conditional with Polymorphism refactoring technique is used to replace conditional logic with polymorphic behavior. This can make the code more maintainable and easier to extend, as well as reducing the complexity of conditional logic. To use the Replace Conditional with Polymorphism technique, we can identify a set of conditionals in the code and create a hierarchy of classes that represent the different cases. We can then use polymorphic behavior to handle the different cases, rather than using conditional logic.# Gang of Four Design Patterns The Gang of Four (GoF) is a group of software engineers who created a seminal book called "Design Patterns: Elements of Reusable Object-Oriented Software". The book describes 23 design patterns that help solve common software design problems. These patterns are divided into three categories: creational patterns, structural patterns, and behavioral patterns. ## Creational Patterns Creational patterns focus on how objects are created and initialized. ### Singleton Pattern The Singleton pattern is used when you want to ensure that only one instance of a class exists in the entire system. This is useful when you have a resource that needs to be shared across multiple objects, like a database connection. ### Factory Pattern Factory Pattern is a creational design pattern that provides an interface for creating objects in a superclass, but allows subclasses to alter the type of objects that will be created. ### Abstract Factory Pattern The Abstract Factory pattern provides an interface for creating families of related or dependent objects without specifying their concrete classes. ### Builder Pattern Builder pattern separates the construction of a complex object from its representation, allowing the same construction process to create various representations.

Structural Patterns

Structural patterns focus on the composition of classes and objects.

Decorator Pattern

Decorator Pattern dynamically adds behaviors to objects at runtime. It is an alternative to subclassing for extending functionality.

Adapter Pattern

Adapter Pattern converts the interface of a class into another interface the client expects. It allows classes to work together that could not otherwise because of incompatible interfaces.

Facade Pattern

Facade Pattern provides a unified interface to a set of interfaces in a subsystem. It defines a higher-level interface that makes the subsystem easier to use.

Proxy Pattern

Proxy Pattern provides a surrogate or placeholder for another object to control access to it.

Behavioral Patterns

Behavioral patterns focus on communication between objects.

Observer Pattern

Observer Pattern defines a one-to-many dependency between objects so that when one object changes state, all its dependents are notified and updated automatically. ### Command Pattern Command Pattern encapsulates a request as an object, thereby letting you parameterize clients with different requests, queue or log requests, and support undoable operations. ### Template Method Pattern Template Method Pattern defines the skeleton of an algorithm in a method, deferring some steps to subclasses. It allows subclasses to redefine certain steps of an algorithm without changing the algorithm's structure. ### Strategy Pattern Strategy Pattern defines a family of algorithms, encapsulates each one, and makes them interchangeable. It lets the algorithm vary independently from clients that use it. By understanding and applying these patterns, you can write more modular, reusable, and maintainable code.

ARCHITECTURAL PATTERNS AND BEST PRACTICES

Architectural patterns provide a proven and well-known way to design and organize large software systems. These patterns provide common structures and approaches that can be used to solve common problems that arise in software architecture. In this subchapter, we will explore some of the most widely used architectural patterns and best practices in Java development. One of the most commonly used architectural patterns is the Model-View-Controller (MVC) pattern. This pattern separates the presentation, logic, and data layers of an application into three distinct components, each with its own responsibilities. The model represents the data and business logic, the view represents the presentation layer, and the controller acts as a mediator between the two. Another popular architectural pattern is the Service-Oriented Architecture (SOA). This pattern defines a set of principles for designing software in which services are the main building blocks. These services represent self-contained components that can be combined to create larger systems. SOA promotes loose coupling, flexibility, and reuse of components. Microservices architecture is another popular pattern that has gained popularity in recent years. This pattern is a variant of SOA that emphasizes the use of small, independent services that work together through APIs. Each service performs a specific task and can be managed independently, allowing for easy scalability and maintenance. When designing software systems, it is essential to follow some best practices that can help ensure a robust, maintainable, and scalable architecture. Following SOLID principles, such as the Single Responsibility Principle and the Open/Closed Principle, can help developers create loosely coupled and easily extensible components. Separating concerns and following design patterns such as Dependency Injection and Inversion of Control can help reduce complexity and make systems more testable. In addition to these principles, it is crucial to consider non-functional requirements, such as performance and security, when designing software systems. Designing for scalability, reducing dependencies, and following secure coding practices can help ensure that software systems are performant and secure. In conclusion, following established architectural patterns and best practices is essential for creating maintainable, scalable, and robust software systems. By separating concerns, following SOLID principles, and considering non-functional requirements, developers can create software systems that are easy to build, test, and maintain over time.

JAVA CODE REFACTORING TECHNIQUES

Refactoring is the process of improving the design and quality of existing code. It involves making changes to the codebase to simplify it, improve readability, and make it more maintainable. The goal of refactoring is to make code easier to understand and modify without changing its functionality. In this subchapter, we will discuss some of the best practices for Java code refactoring.

Why Refactor Java Code?

Over time, software systems tend to become more complex and harder to maintain. As new features are added and bugs are fixed, the codebase can become cluttered and difficult to work with. This is where refactoring comes in. By refactoring code, developers can: - Improve code readability and maintainability - Reduce complexity and improve software quality - Eliminate code smells and improve code hygiene - Increase testability and decrease the likelihood of introducing bugs - Increase developer productivity and decrease development time

When Should You Refactor Your Java Code?

Refactoring should be an ongoing process throughout the development cycle. However, there are a few specific times when refactoring is particularly valuable: - When adding a new feature: Before adding a new feature to the codebase, it is often helpful to refactor the existing code to make it easier to work with. This can save time and reduce the likelihood of introducing bugs. - When fixing a bug: When fixing a bug, it's a good idea to refactor the surrounding code to make it more maintainable and prevent future bugs. - During code reviews: Code reviews are a great time to identify areas of the codebase that could benefit from refactoring. Addressing these issues during code reviews can improve the overall quality of the codebase.

Types of Refactoring Techniques

There are many types of refactoring techniques that can be used when working with Java code. Here are a few common ones: - Extract Method: This technique involves taking a block of code and extracting it into a separate method. This can improve code readability and make it easier to modify the extracted code in the future. - Rename Variable/Method/Class: This technique involves changing the name of a variable, method, or class to better reflect its purpose. This can improve code readability and make it easier to understand. - Replace Magic Number with Symbolic Constant: This technique involves replacing hard-coded numbers with symbolic constants. This can improve code readability and make it easier to modify the code in the future. - Inline Method: This technique involves taking a method and inlining its code into the calling method. This can reduce code complexity and improve performance. - Extract Interface/Class: This technique involves taking a class and extracting an interface or superclass from it. This can improve code modularity and make it easier to work with.

Best Practices for Refactoring Java Code

When refactoring Java code, there are a few best practices to keep in mind: - Write Unit Tests: Before refactoring code, it's a good idea to have a suite of unit tests in place.

This can help ensure that the refactoring does not introduce bugs. - Refactor in Small Steps: Refactoring should be done in small, incremental steps. Each refactoring should improve the codebase without changing its functionality. This can make it easier to identify and fix issues. - Keep the Code Working: Code should be kept working throughout the refactoring process. This can be achieved by ensuring that tests continue to pass after each refactoring step. - Use Refactoring Tools: There are many tools available for automating the refactoring process in Java. These tools can help ensure that refactoring is done consistently and efficiently. In conclusion, refactoring is an essential part of the software development process. By following best practices and using the right techniques, developers can simplify code, improve maintainability, and reduce bugs.

Chapter 10: Java Performance Optimization

As a Java programmer, it's important to understand how to optimize your code to run as efficiently as possible. In this chapter, we will cover several key aspects of Java performance optimization, including memory management, profiling, and tuning.

SUBCHAPTER 10.1: JAVA MEMORY MANAGEMENT AND PERFORMANCE

Java memory management is an important aspect of performance optimization. When Java applications run, they create objects in memory. If these objects are not properly managed, they can cause performance issues such as excessive memory usage and garbage collection. One way to optimize memory usage is to use data structures that are optimized for the size and type of data being stored. For example, if you are storing a large number of small objects, it might be more efficient to use an array or primitive type like int or double, rather than an object like Integer. Another way to optimize memory usage is to enable and configure Java's garbage collector. The garbage collector is responsible for freeing up memory that is no longer being used by an application. By configuring the garbage collector appropriately, you can ensure that memory is being used efficiently.

SUBCHAPTER 10.2: PROFILING AND TUNING JAVA APPLICATIONS

Profiling is the process of analyzing an application's performance to identify bottlenecks and areas where performance can be improved. There are several tools available for profiling Java applications, including the built-in Java Virtual Machine (JVM) tool, JVisualVM, and third-party tools like JProfiler and YourKit. Once you have identified performance issues in your application, you can start tuning it to improve performance. This may involve making changes to the code, such as optimizing loops or using more efficient algorithms, or tweaking JVM settings such as garbage collection parameters or memory allocation.

SUBCHAPTER 10.3: BEST PRACTICES FOR JAVA PERFORMANCE OPTIMIZATION

There are several best practices that Java programmers can follow to optimize performance. Some of these include: - Use efficient data structures and algorithms - Minimize object creation and keep objects small - Use immutable objects where possible - Use caching to avoid unnecessary computations - Avoid excessive synchronization - Use profiling tools to identify performance bottlenecks - Continuously monitor and tune application performance By following these best practices, Java programmers can ensure that their applications are running as efficiently as possible and delivering optimal performance.

JAVA MEMORY MANAGEMENT AND PERFORMANCE

Efficient memory management in Java is essential for optimal application performance. The Java Virtual Machine (JVM) is responsible for managing memory allocation and deallocation automatically, which simplifies application development, but can also result in performance trade-offs. Java uses a garbage collector to manage memory allocation. The garbage collector periodically scans the heap, identifying objects that are no longer being used, and freeing up their memory. However, improperly managing memory in Java can result in performance issues such as excessive garbage collection, memory leaks, and OutOfMemoryErrors. Therefore, it is important to properly understand how memory is managed in Java. Java memory is divided into two main regions: the stack and the heap. The stack is used to store local variables and method calls, while the heap is used to store objects and arrays. The JVM manages the heap memory through several algorithms. The most common one is the mark-and-sweep algorithm, which scans the heap for objects that are no longer being used and frees up their memory. To optimize memory management and prevent performance issues, Java developers can use several tools and techniques such as: - Using object pooling to reuse objects instead of creating new ones - Setting appropriate JVM memory parameters such as the minimum and maximum heap size and garbage collection options - Avoiding unnecessary object creation by using primitives instead of objects where possible - Implementing efficient data structures and algorithms - Using profiling and monitoring tools to identify memory leaks and performance bottlenecks By employing proper memory management strategies, Java applications can achieve optimal performance and responsiveness.

PROFILING AND TUNING JAVA APPLICATIONS

When it comes to developing high-performance Java applications, profiling and tuning are critical tasks. Profiling helps you identify performance bottlenecks in your code, while tuning helps you optimize and improve the overall performance of your application. There are numerous tools available for profiling Java applications, including built-in tools like Java VisualVM and third-party tools like JProfiler and YourKit. These tools allow you to monitor CPU usage, memory usage, and other important metrics, which can help you identify specific areas of your code that are causing performance issues. Once you've identified performance bottlenecks in your code, you can start the tuning process. Tuning involves making changes to your code or configuration settings to improve performance. For example, you might optimize frequently used algorithms, reduce memory usage, or adjust thread settings to better utilize available resources. It's important to note that tuning should always be done in a methodical and iterative manner. Before making any changes, be sure to measure the current performance of your application using your profiling tool. Then, make small changes and measure the effect on performance. This approach will help you identify which changes are most effective and avoid introducing new performance issues. Overall, profiling and tuning are essential skills for anyone building high-performance Java applications. By using the right tools and following a methodical approach, you can optimize your code for maximum performance and deliver the best possible user experience.

www.ingramcontent.com/pod-product-compliance
Lightning Source LLC
Chambersburg PA
CBHW070656220526
45466CB00001B/457